A Letter to Dua

Roya Khalili

Jun/2024

© 2024 Roya Khalili

All rights reserved. No part of this book may be reproduced or transmitted in any form or by any means, electronic or mechanical, including photocopying, recording, or by any information storage and retrieval system, without permission in writing from the publisher, except by a reviewer who may quote brief passages in a review.

ISBN: 9781068243806

For information, address:

[Rulikhalili27@gmail.com]

For Women, Life, Freedom

Foreword

I didn't write these letters for the world.
I wrote them for one small soul, my daughter, Dua.

They came to life in quiet moments:
when I was afraid; when I cried from longing and despair, when I felt proud, and when I was joyful.

I was alone in a foreign country, and that loneliness became both the greatest gift and the hardest test of my life.

The only thing that brought peace to my soul was the heartbeat inside me.

When I started writing to Dua, something in me began to change. She helped me face my pain and showed me a softer way to be with myself.

I felt things I'd never felt before. Writing became a quiet place where I could go somewhere safe, where I could connect to the love and trust she was already giving me.

Dua gave me the courage to write my feelings.

I was once a frightened woman, carrying the weight of a lonely child I used to be. But with Dua growing inside me, I began to heal.

Maybe she'll never understand what she did for me.
Maybe she'll never read all of these letters.
Maybe she'll forget most of them.

But they lived inside me.
And maybe that's enough.

—Roya

In Persian (Farsi) and many other languages, 'Dua' means prayer or supplication, involving a sincere and wholehearted request to God or a higher power for guidance, blessings, or assistance.
This practice is shared across various cultures and religions.

The First Letter: Welcome

As you travel to embrace the world, I wait eagerly, ready to hold you in the arms of a woman whose only refuge is the God of the heavens. You have chosen me as your parent; this woman that I am: a woman both strange and solitary. A woman who carries her wounds like a cross upon her shoulders, and who never knows from which path a miracle may arrive.

My soul carries deep scars. I have known the pain of separation, yet even with a weary body I can still greet the trees in the cool of autumn and weep for hours over the death of a small bird. Through the years, I have learned how to stand firm in the battle of life; with perseverance and love; and you have chosen this very woman.

From the moment I felt your presence, all the darkness disappeared. You shine like the sun and illuminate me from within. When I imagine you, I see beauty in its purest form, as if loneliness had never been a part of me; and never will be again.

I wish to begin with you a journey through uncertainty. You are a breath of heaven within an earthly body, and each time I feel your presence inside me I remember how God breathes Himself into us so that love may continue on this earth.

If one day you become a poet, you will taste the healing essence of poetry through the trials of life. Life is not a field of tests; it is a path toward awakening. Each time your heart breaks, a piece of the wall of your ego will fall, and a light of truth will shine within you. There is meaning in pain, and in the silence of tears, the voice of God can be heard.

I will guide you to follow your dreams among the stars, without fear of falling. My heart is filled with joy, for I know you are on your way to me. I will teach you what I have learned about being human; and I believe you will surpass me, my mother, and her mother before her. You are the continuation of a light made of love, simplicity, and pure beauty.

One day you will understand that the woman who speaks to you now is the same one you will call Mother.

The Second Letter: Evangelism

They say that in the Realm of Souls, the spirits once stood before God, and He asked, "Am I not your Lord?" All replied, "Yes." You too were among them when you whispered, "Send me into the arms of a woman who knows the path of love." And I became that woman; not by chance, but by your choice.

I do not know whether you were in the world of Barzakh or in the highest heaven; I only know that you were a small drop from the vast ocean of the Holy Spirit who became a guest in the house of my heart. One day, you read me like a poem, and your voice became a song in my ears, telling me that you had chosen me to walk beside you on this journey toward Him.

From the boundless sea of souls, you chose me; to hear the voice of God through my lips, to learn love through the wounds of my heart, and to understand through my gaze that suffering is the path that leads to light.

I heard you; your voice and your presence; when the appointed time arrived. I had never imagined that the hour of revelation could be announced to a woman so lost in thought that she stared at a squirrel in the street.

Each day, I spoke to the voice within me, asking me to answer its call. I told you I would try to find the path that leads us together, even though I myself was lost in the twists of life, moving from the alley of yesterday into the street of tomorrow. Then, suddenly, you found me. You took form within me. You blossomed, and the promised day arrived.

No birth is ever an accident. Every soul chooses its own path consciously; to enter a particular body, in a specific place, at a destined time; to learn a lesson that can be taught only through that journey. You came to complete me, to continue me, to let the cycle of creation repeat itself within us. I became the embrace, and you became the breath. I became the earth, and you blossomed.

We have been companions since eternity. Our souls were born from the same light and, by divine promise, have found each other again. The light of the Creator's love shone upon us. To you, He granted the grace to be the herald, and to me, the gift of creation; so that both of us might be redeemed. I heard the sound of your prayer and answered that heavenly call; for whatever comes from the Beloved is always good.

From Roya, the woman you will one day call Mother.

The Third Letter: A Single Grape

I am the pure vine,
and in my veins flows
the crimson wine of you.
There is no pain within my heart—
only the ache of being alone.

You are the bud that appeared
upon my branch in summer,
like the first blossom of spring,
like fire
in the heart of winter.

You gave fruit,
so my heart would not lose its way.
You became the shelter of my life,
my love,
my sleeping beauty.

O grape of my heart,
your scent is the fragrance of paradise.
Your sacred name is written
on the tablet of my heart—
a prayer
scribed by God.

With you, the wine is eternal.
O pure Shiraz,
from you I make my love
warm as the moment of flight.

You came to build a bridge
from God to the heart of home,
so that I would no longer be a stranger
and you could make your nest
inside my soul.

The Fourth Letter: The Visit

Every day, I count the moments, longing for the clock to finally reach the hour of our meeting. Yet time moves against my will, rolling slowly, as if conspiring against my desire and refusing to close the distance between us.

What are you to me? Are you a verse woven from the threads of poetry? A radiant sun that brightens my days? Perhaps a fleeting glimpse of the divine, or an idol sculpted from the shape of my longing. You flow through me like a quiet stream, passing through my being and reshaping my soul.

When I finally hold you in my arms, I will ask: What twist in the branch of fate made you choose me? Before you, I was a poet; after you, I became a bird. You changed the form of my existence, and now I am no longer myself; I am you.

God poured a fragment of His own presence into your body and my soul. From that moment, I was no longer merely flesh and bone. You became the bearer of the secret of life; a bridge between heaven and earth.

Each day I close my eyes and meet you again. You ripple within me, and I move to the rhythm of your presence. You blossom inside me, and I become spring. Our destinies are woven together.

    They say there is a hidden bond between mother and child: what science calls "shared particles," and what mystics name "unity of spirit." Every cell of you within me carries a remembrance of God, traveling from my body into yours to remind me that the boundary between us is only an illusion.

    My blood courses through your veins, just as my soul flows within yours. We have risen like two waves from the same sea; and no matter how far apart we drift, we will always hear each other's voice in the depths of our being. There are pieces of you within me, and reflections of me within you. Perhaps that is the eternal truth: that you and I are one.

The Fifth Letter: Whisper

You come to me each day like a quiet whisper, and every morning I wake with the longing to see you. I miss the day when my heart cried out that you had entered me, when I somehow knew, in a way beyond words, that I wanted you. Every day I miss you. Every day, I am restless for your presence.

In every part of my being, I feel the gentle rhythm of your movements within me. You are the meaning of all my dreams, the very shape of courage, and the purest form of love I have ever known. You are so beautiful that sometimes I fear my eyes will not be strong enough to behold you.

You remind me of the first time I fell in love. I fell in love in the summer. You, too, will be born in summer. From that moment on, with every summer that returns, I will fall in love again.

I have tasted many kinds of love; the wildness of passion that one day you, too, may come to know, and the quiet, truthful loves that carry no trace of ego or possession.

Love is the first language of God. Before a single word was spoken, before any light was born, it was love that set the world into motion. But love has many faces.

Through the journey of the soul, it appears in countless forms so that the spirit may learn the path from earth to heaven.

There is love in caring for animals, in cherishing trees and orange blossoms, in loving your mother and father, and in the sweetness of a lover's first kiss.

At first, love is earthly; that familiar pull that begins with a look, a smile, or a presence. This kind of love, though born in the world, is not false; it is a bridge from the surface to the depths. Through human love, one learns how to truly see beauty.

Yet among all forms of love, there is one that stands above the rest; a complete love, a divine love; where the lover sees God in the act of loving another and does not forget humanity while worshipping the divine. For both are made of the same light, two reflections of a single truth.

And you, my little answered prayer, are the newest form of love I have ever known. Today, I am more in love than ever.

The Sixth Letter: The Basin of Life

I seek refuge in you from the world outside. You have not yet reached my embrace, yet the wounds within me have already begun to heal. You have given me the power to feel life again. The air I breathe; the air we now share; is no longer ordinary. It carries the scent of heaven into my weary soul. The body I share with you has found new life in the blessing of your presence.

You drift within me, floating in the sacred waters of my being; a small, shining fish swimming in circles, singing softly to the sun the poems you already know by heart. Your quiet movements ripple through me like prayer, and every wave you make reminds me that life begins where stillness once was.

They say that at the moment of birth, a child believes it is dying; though in truth, it is being born. Like a fish in an aquarium who mistake the vastness of the sea for death, do not fear, my daughter, when the time comes to leave the waters inside me. Every death is followed by a birth.

Your birth, my Dua, will be the first great lesson of your life. Know this: nothing in existence is ever quite what it seems. Seek truth within what appears real, for reality is what happens, but truth is what hides behind it.

To understand this mystery will be the beginning of your soul's awakening. Everything you see in this world is but a shadow of something deeper. One day, you will realize that reality itself is only a stage upon which truth reveals its face; and that realization will be the light shining in your heart.

The Seventh Letter: The Secret of the Red Rose

You live within me, and that gives meaning to my life. After you, every thought feels empty, and every desire is nothing more than longing without purpose. I am so bound to you that separation seems impossible.

How did you bring this change upon me? It feels as though the whole world has begun to shine. You are the shape of a miracle; pure arrival, pure being. You dwell inside me, and I love this shared body of ours to the edge of madness.

You are the small God within me, the one who appeared in my solitude. After you, miracles can only be understood through you: words and syllables find their meaning only in your presence. Stars, to me, will be your eyes. The sky, your gaze.

You are the Holy Spirit who descended into me in a moment of prayer and need, so that I might learn once again through the vision of your beholding. It feels as though I have been given another chance to live; to heal the open wounds and the quiet anger buried deep inside me.

My daughter, I will tell you the secret of the sun and of the red roses, and of the love found in eyes that see only beauty. For the world is not as it is; it is as we see it.

Colours and shapes are mirrors of the soul; every heart creates a world made of its own light. If your eyes are filled with love, everything will bathe in the meaning of light. If your sight grows weary and lifeless, even a flower will lose its trace of heaven.

Life must be seen anew; not with the eyes of the body, but with the eyes of the heart, where reality passes and truth remains.

My daughter, Dua, one day you will understand that to see is itself a form of being born. Each time your gaze is renewed, a new world is born with it.

Let the eyes of your heart see love before they judge, and then you will know that the world is reborn through you; that you are a mirror of the light that shines by the name of life. Many live without love: breathing, but not truly alive. Love, my Dua, is the secret of survival; the mystery of why humanity continues to exist.

"A life without love is not worth counting. Love is the water of life; let it flow into your heart and soul."

~ Rumi

The Eighth Letter: Polish

My daughter, stay where you are; within me. Let us go on living together in this shared body, for as long as time allows.

The miracle of your existence has melted and reshaped something inside me, something I never thought could change. I am no longer who I was; that other self has vanished, and I do not miss her. Perhaps this is what love truly means: to never long for what we once were.

Love, my Dua, is what polishes the human soul. It refines us, giving our being a quiet gleam. But love is not peace; it is fire: a fire that burns not to destroy, but to cleanse. From the beginning of time, we humans were made from this same fire, shaped in its furnace, just as raw clay must be fired before it becomes strong and whole. Without pain, there is only coldness. Without burning, there is no form.

Love burns. Love hurts deeply. Yet without this burning, the human heart remains unformed. Even stones, under heat, grow firm. I believe, my child, that love is what makes us divine; for among all creatures, only we are able to love with reason as well as heart.

When a person falls in love, they shed their shell and break through the walls of their ego. They step naked into the madness of love, and kindness becomes their second skin. In their eyes, suffering gains meaning; in their burning, light is born.

Remember this, my daughter: every pain that comes from love is proof that your soul is alive. Love burns the heart so that it may rise from the dust of repetition and turn into light. Then you will understand; pain is the womb from which the soul is born, the place where truth emerges from within reality.

The Ninth Letter: Arrived

It feels as though a light has been breathed into the roots of my longing, so that the world may pass through me and reach you.

You have made me new again. With your coming, I have left my fears behind and emptied myself of all that once was.

They say that when a newborn emerges from the darkness into the light, the world itself is born again.

With your birth, I too have been reborn; as if I am meant to see the world now through the horizon of your eyes.

I have heard that a woman who gives birth becomes a partner in God's work, for she brings existence from the unseen into the seen.

In the face of every newborn, God reveals a new image of Himself, and the first cry of a child echoes the sound of "Be"; the very word by which creation began.

I do not know how long I have missed home, but from you, I can smell the scent of my homeland. When I hold you in my arms, it feels as though I am cradling all of Iran.

Before you came, I was left behind at a station, between a train with no path and a destination long forgotten.

But now that you are here, the chapter of my joy and wonder smells of rain once more.

Every breath of yours carries the fragrance of Shiraz streets on the first day of spring.

I cannot tell whether the orange blossoms borrow their scent from you, or if you yourself are the fragrance of fresh rosewater.

I should have named you Wine, for you are so intoxicating that you make the verses of my poems lose their balance. And I can find no rhyme for your innocence.

Dua, my doe-eyed daughter, you stepped softly into the garden of a woman's heart; a woman who, in the drought of love, had tied her hopes to the heavens.

I was that woman, the one who prayed; and you were my answered prayer.

Welcome, my child, to the book of this woman's life.

The Tenth Letter: Luminance in the Eyes

Before you, I had never sworn by anyone's eyes, nor tasted honey from another's lips. How newly you must have come from paradise, for the scent of God's own hand still lingers between the strands of your dark hair.

What remembrance did He place in your eyes, that poetry drips from their corners and this woman; this heart—has gone mad with your gaze? You have become the verse of my heart: "He who answers the distressed when they call upon Him, and removes their suffering."

My Dua, your glances are wondrous, tender, divine. You are the Light of My Eyes, the small God within my home, and I am left in awe of all the radiance you have brought into my house. My daughter, to give my life for the eyes of a gazelle like yours would be the sweetest death.

I've written so many poems for your eyes
that your eyes became poetry themselves.
Where could I ever hide from them
when the verse of your gaze
is water upon the fire of every rhyme?

Again, the gentle deer of your glance
has wandered into the garden of my poems,
and my verses, dazzled by you,
have turned white.

The Eleventh Letter: Rose from the Fire

There is a phoenix hidden within every human being; a bird made of fire and patience that burns only to be born again.

Life, too, is the same. Every burning leads to a rising; every pain opens a door to light. No birth comes without ashes. Just as gold is purified in the fire, the soul finds meaning through suffering.

If one day you feel yourself collapsing inward, remember the phoenix that rose from the heart of the flames. Allow yourself to burn; not to be destroyed, but to become. True living is to live like a phoenix: to die many times, and to be born each time more beautiful than before.

These days I find myself becoming more and more like my mother; a phoenix in her own right. It is as though another woman has taken shelter inside my eyes: a woman both proud and gentle, strong and serene. A woman who has bloomed once again from her own ashes.

We may not look alike, but the gift of flight is the inheritance she left within me.

I am Roya Khalili, born on February 7th, 1990, in Shiraz, Iran; the daughter of a woman who was reborn through fire and rose stronger every time she burned. And you, Dua Babaei, born on August 26th, 2020, in Bournemouth, England; you are the child of a woman who has always risen from the flames with steadfast grace.

Know this, my Dua: within you, too, a free bird sleeps, waiting for its moment to ignite.

That is our legacy to you. Believe that after every hardship comes ease, and know that even the fire can become your teacher.

My daughter, child of fire and light, remember that burning is not destruction—it is birth. The fire does not consume you; it shapes you. From every flame, new wings will grow upon the soul.

Dua, my little phoenix, this time you have been born from within me. I will wait for your blossoming, for the wonders of your flight, for the way you will transform the world inside you. You will fight, you will make peace, and one day you will give birth to a phoenix of your own.

Perhaps one day, like me, you will see your mother's face reflected behind your eyes, and hear her song within your heart; the song of a freed phoenix whispering to you: *When fear comes, do not be afraid.*

Rise. Continue your path. And say it aloud, with all your strength: long live being a woman.

The Twelfth Letter: Balm

I touch the smooth tresses of your hair—
like night
in the heart of a forest.

You are the princess
in tales never told.

In your presence, my soul catches flame—
a blaze of radiance, quiet and full.

A bundle of wheat
rests upon your eyelids.

Your eyes...
a road winding into the unknown.

You close them.
Then open.

And spring arrives—
dancing light
blooming from within.

I drown in your smile—
soft, magnetic,
full of hunger.

You are the sweetness
of first love.
You are a prayer,
a balm
for this aching body.

The Thirteenth Letter: Remember the Flight

Birds grow up and leave their nests. Their dreams rise higher than we ever imagined. You, too, will no longer be the tiny being I once held in my arms. Our paths will one day separate. We will no longer share one body, and I will come to realize that you were never truly mine. I was only the temporary guardian of a light that passed from God through me and into you.

You live in my house; but, in truth, you dwell within the vastness of my heart. As I folded the little clothes that no longer fit you, a storm rose inside me and my tears fell like the first rain of spring. Time rushes forward. You grow older, and I fear that I still haven't said everything I need to tell you.

Remember the flight; the bird is mortal. One day, you will soar: radiant, fearless, a woman of your own making. But in my eyes, you will always be that 2,500-gram girl who taught me how to love without condition—who showed me both the fragility of my own soul and the divine strength that lives through you. That understanding, my daughter, is what leads me to humility and to love.

I swear upon your innocent eyes that I will be grateful every single day. I will remain by your side, wherever life may take you. I will stand behind you and whisper: rise again from the very place you fall, and grow stronger from the moments that made you feel weak.

Even your enemies, my love, can become the cause of good. Those who wish to see you fall may bring you to the very edge of the cliff, but you must open your wings and fly against the pull of their gravity.

The Fourteenth Letter: Homeland

Since the day you arrived and brought light into my life, longing has quietly departed. When I hold you against my chest, it feels as though I am embracing my homeland. When I breathe you in, your scent carries the memory of a small fragment of my childhood; a feeling that takes me back to a place I once belonged to completely. It is like the soft morning breeze during the spring exams, our home in Dasht Chanar, first grade in the year 1997.

But your hair reminds me of the nights in Tehran; nights of youth and restlessness, nights of love and surrender. When I touch your presence, I forget that I live in a foreign land.

One day, when you read these letters, they may sound strange to you. England will be your homeland, English your first language, and Christmas your celebration. Yet you are fortunate, my daughter, for you will grow between two cultures, two skies.

But for me, who live far from home, you are the shape of my homeland; like my cats, the ones who once sought shelter in our house from the streets; like my old bedroom in my mother's home, the refuge of all my sorrows. You are the voice of my grandmother in our last conversation, and the echo of Arash, who flew away from me too soon. Sometimes you become Shiraz itself; Mulla Sadra Street; or you resemble my aunts, Sima and Sahar, when I miss them deeply.

Dua, when I breathe you in, all my sadness fades away. My mother once told me I was like water: "If you stay still too long, you will turn to mud." And now I say to you: You too are like water; you pour over the fire of my longing and cool my heart. Since you came, I have begun to flow again. Whatever in me had grown stagnant in exile, you washed away like spring rain, making me alive and new once more.

Ah, my daughter of restless nights, how deeply grateful I am for you.

The Fifteenth Letter: A Lullaby

Dua Babaei—
little girl,
sitting quietly
with her doll.

Sometimes she laughs
at balloons.
Sometimes she sings
with butterflies.

Her hand—
like the wing
of an angel.

Her eyes hold
a kind of soft magic.

Dua Babaei,
you are our daughter,
and your very being
brings goodness.

Your cheeks—
like fresh pomegranate—
sweet and full of colours.

Your hair,
soft and wavy—
calm and proud
like your father,
but with your mother's eyes.

The Sixteenth Letter: Eternal Spring Tree

We journeyed around the sun together, leaving traces of our presence across all four seasons. You grew beside me, and I witnessed a miracle; the miracle of a woman whose driest branches blossomed green again. When hardship dried the soil of my homeland and weakened its roots, I left and planted myself once more on a vast and unfamiliar island. And, then, you became my fruit; the harvest of all my pain and hope.

Now you stand tall like a proud cedar: strong, radiant, and full of life. Every day, you astonish me. Through you, I live again; the life that was once taken from me has returned. What a second life you have gifted me; the day you bloomed on my lap and turned everything green again.

My only wish is that in your memory my smile and these letters will remain. If one day you feel alone among people, or find yourself caught in the autumn of your soul, or shivering in the shadow of winter, remember our shared journey. You are never alone. I will be in the wind, in the scent of rain, and in the quiet of your midnight dreams.

No distance can ever build a wall between our hearts. I continue within you; in the rhythm of your heartbeat and in the light that shines through your eyes. Whenever you feel lonely, place your hand upon your chest. I am there, still beating.

You awakened something new within me, and together we became spring. Without you, I am no longer a tree; without me, you do not bloom. We are intertwined, like ivy wrapping around a tree and drawing life from its trunk.

I am here; your poem, your shelter, your shoulder to lean on, your embrace for the days when you feel trapped, and your hand for tenderness. Always. You will forever remain a part of my heart, flowing through me for as long as breath lives within my chest.

The Seventeenth Letter: Dua, a Healer

You fell, and your knees were scraped. I wasn't there; not at the moment when you needed me to soothe your pain, to hold you in my arms so that you wouldn't feel alone.

Dua, please don't do that to me again. Don't be angry with me anymore. Never tell me that you don't love me, or that you don't want to speak to me.

Don't take your hands away from the heart you once healed.

In those few days when your gentle hands withdrew from my chest, the wounds I thought had healed began to bleed again. You did it because you were afraid—afraid of being alone. And, yes, life without someone there to kiss your wounds is frightening. I understand that fear well.

I knew it long before you; throughout my childhood, my youth, the years before you came. That same fear spilled into you, and it made you restless. You had every right to be upset, because I had promised you something I could not always keep: that you would never have to feel what I once felt.

But Dua, my healer, life does not always follow the path we plan.

I thought and thought until my heart ached. I bled inside, like a bird trapped in its cage, terrified that you might believe you no longer had me. Perhaps it was the tenderness of your soul that stirred such a storm in mine. You are like me; strong as a mountain, yet fragile as snow; and this truth has stolen my sleep.

My cherry blossom, the world is not kind to sensitive souls. I fell many times, and no one ever tended to my wounds. And now my greatest fear is that you might live through that same loneliness I once knew.

Sleep has left me. I've lost my appetite. You were angry with me, and I with myself.

Never again, my child, feel alone while I exist. If you are near me and still feel loneliness, I will drown in an ocean of sorrow; like a whale that dies of love when it loses its mate.

If you ever feel alone, I will lose my words. My poems will vanish. My letters will be left behind, forgotten under the rain of my own tears.

Don't tell me not to talk to you. What will happen to all these anxious words if they can't reach you? What will become of the poems I haven't yet written for you, or the sentences filled with love that still wait to be spoken?

Let me speak to you, Dua. I want to tell you that even when you say, "I don't love you," even when you tell me not to speak to you, I am proud of you. The moment you pull your hands away from my heart, I feel an unexpected pride; because I realize that you are braver than I ever was, and that I had managed to teach you something I never truly learned myself.

Draw your boundaries. Define your lines. Shout. Blame me. Be wild. Be light. But never feel alone with me.

Don't take your hands away from my heart, Dua. From my wounds still drips the quiet pain of abandonment.

The Eighteenth Letter: Parallel World

My daughter, sometimes when you close your eyes, another world begins; a place where time no longer matters; and there, somewhere between light and sound, I sit beside you once more.

They say this world is not all that exists and that beyond this veil lies an endless series of mirrors, each reflecting the other, and that within each reflection we live another version of ourselves.

Perhaps in another world you are the mother holding me in your arms, and I am the small child resting in your lap. Perhaps in that world, we both have wings and fly across a light that beats from the same heart. Mystics say that every soul lives in many realms; in the world of earth, in the world of imagination, and in the world of light. We are awake to only one of them, but the invisible thread of love binds them all together.

So if one day you dream of being somewhere unfamiliar; in a city you do not recognize, surrounded by nameless faces; and yet you feel a deep peace, know that in that other world, I was there with you. We are two reflections of one light, shining through two mirrors of existence. Wherever you are, I am there too;

in the whisper of a breeze, in a glimmer of light, or within a gentle song.

Dua, no distance can ever separate souls that have risen from the same source. If in this world you ever miss me, close your eyes and, in the silence, whisper "Mother." And from that other world, I will answer you; softly, always near.

The Nineteenth Letter: Wound

You glimpsed
the depths of my soul.

You touched
the wounds hidden within me—
and you healed them,
Dua.

Look:
I treasure these scars.

These wounds,
lying deep
at the core of my chest,
sometimes reopen—

not to break me,
but to remind me
of the courage it took
to survive
this life.

The Twentieth Letter: Metamorphosis

Last night, as always, when a nightmare found you, you sought refuge in my arms. But this time, something was different. Your face glowed beneath the soft red light of the lamp, shining like the moon. God seems to have gathered all the beauty of the world within you—your long, velvety lashes, your delicate nose, and those wide eyes that reach even into my dreams. Your lips, still shaped like flower buds, carried the sweetness of wine even in the trembling dark. Your hair, flowing like strands of wheat over your shoulders, shimmered gently in the shadows.

As I held you, I suddenly realized that you no longer fit in my arms. Your legs have grown long; your head no longer rests easily in my hands. You have outgrown my frame. Time has passed so quickly. You are no longer the tiny, fragile being I once carried close to my heart.

You are growing, and that growth is also the expansion of my own being. You will drift farther from me. And yet, the farther you go, the deeper you will live within me.

Return whenever you wish. This embrace is a home without borders or time, built not of earth, but of love. Its door will never close, for in my heart, a light will always be burning to guide you home.

The Twenty-First Letter: A Letter to Dua

One day, we will find our way back to each other. I write this letter for you—for the day when you are a teenager: bold, beautiful, and full of confidence. When you reach the age when my thoughts seem smaller than your feelings, and my experiences appear less valuable than your ideas, remember that we already know how to stay connected. There are paths between us that will always lead back to our hearts.

Dua, look at the stars. Years ago, I passed among them in the solitude of my nights, searching for a light to guide me forward. But you, my love, don't need to walk through darkness; it is enough for you to simply look at them and enjoy their glow. My life was a story of being left behind and forgotten, but yours should be a tale of peace, belonging, and arrival.

I wish I could be the wild thorns around your being, protecting your heart from anything that dares to leave a mark upon it. I wish I could light a flame within you—a light no darkness could ever extinguish—to guard you against every sorrow and pain.

But people will sometimes hurt you. They will wound your soul—with words, with neglect, with ignorance. And yet, it will not be the end of the world.

Remember, we are like ivy; forever intertwined and forever connected. No distance can separate us, for our roots are woven into the same soil. Come to me, cry to me, tell me about the wounds that have scarred your spirit, about the days when the world felt too heavy to bear. Even if I don't always know how to listen, I will open my heart completely to you, because no sound in this world is more sacred to me than the sound of your voice.

The Twenty-Second Letter: I Am Not My Words

I am not like my words.
I am more like the sky
when it's half-clouded—
uncertain, shifting,
but honest.

Don't look for me
in what I say.
Find me
inside my poems.

I am not as strong
as my words make me seem.
I am like the scent of heartbreak
clinging to every line.

But if I ever speak of love—
believe me.

When I am sad,
I carry your name—Dua—
the way a cross is carried.
Not lightly,
but with devotion.

I followed you
through every path,
step by step.

And oh—
what joy it was
to share the sweetness
of having you.

About the Author

Roya Khalili is a British–Iranian writer whose work blends poetry, personal reflection, and emotional honesty. Her writing gently explores love, identity, motherhood, and the quiet transformations that shape the human spirit.

Born in Iran and now based in the UK, Roya carries the echoes of a difficult childhood; marked by separation, rejection, and the silent traumas of growing up in a culture where emotional wounds often go unseen. Writing became her sanctuary, a way to survive and to make sense of pain. She began composing poems as early as the age of three, finding in language the shelter she couldn't find elsewhere.

Motherhood opened a new door in her life; one that led her toward profound love and the courage to face her deepest scars. Through her daughter, Dua, she discovered a path of healing: to meet her inner child with compassion, to befriend the pain, and to transform it into tenderness.

Roya believes that reaching out a hand to one's own trauma requires a rare kind of strength; a sacred act of bravery. For her, motherhood became both the wound and the cure, the breaking and the becoming.

A Letter to Dua is her first published collection. A tender offering of letters and poems from a mother to her daughter, written across the threshold between pain and love.